Moslem Girls' Training Guide

Divinely Prepared for

The Sisters' Auxiliary of
The Moorish Science Temple of America

This Guide is the Property of

_____

Moslem Girls' Training Guide

Divinely Prepared for

The Sisters' Auxiliary of
The Moorish Science Temple of America

© 2014
Califa Media ™

Originally published 1928
Sis. Augustus Bey
Moorish Science Temple of America

Revised & Edited by
Sis. Tauheedah S. Najee-Ullah El

TABLE OF CONTENTS

Acknowledgement & Gratitude	i.
Preface	ii.
Editors Note	iii.
Introduction	1
The Moslem Girls' Training & General Civilization Class	
• Instruction on The Law of Women in Islam	3
Sisters in Auxiliary	6
The Nationalization of a People	
• One of the many programs of the Divine Mission of the Prophet of Ali, Allah's Prophet	7
A Few Good Moors	8
How to Dress	10
Laws and Instructions	
• Moslem Rules	12
Orders of the Sisters in Auxiliary	14
Proper Attitude	15
• Language	16
• Conversation	17
• Some Facts About "Gossip"	18
• How NOT To Use Our Tongues	19
• How We SHOULD Use Our Tongues	19
Posture	20
• Mannerisms	21
• Manners	21
The Dangers of Being Overweight	23
• Dangers of Inactivity	23
• Overweight Develops Heart Trouble	24
Some Great Tips on Caring For Our Hair	25
• Tips on Combing and Brushing the Hair	25
• "Make it Yourself Moorish Care Products	26

TABLE OF CONTENTS cont.

Moslem Girls' Training & Sisters' Auxiliary	
• Student Class Creed	27
• Ways and Reasons to be Successful on the Job	27
100 Do's and Don'ts of the Moslem Girls' Training & Sisters' Auxiliary	28
How to Keep House	
• A Thirty Day Program that will Turn Your House Into a Moslem Home	33
• Get Rid of Clutter	33
• Day 1	34
The Moslem's Courtship	35
Sisters' Auxiliary	
• Student Class Creed	36
The Uplifting of Fallen Humanity	37
How to Take Care of Your Husband	38
• Comfort Him	38
• Appreciate Him	39
• Forgive Him	40
• Be Clean and Beautiful	41
• Think of No Other Man	41
• Be Wise in Dealing With In-Laws	42
• Do Not Look For Shortcomings	43
• Don't Be Suspicious	44
• Help Him Avoid Pitfalls	45
• The Divided House	47
Moorish Girls' Training	
• How to Rear Our Children: Notes to Remember	49
• Obedience	50
• Remember Lot's Wife	54
Temple Manners	56
Mother Love	57
The Law of Islamism in America	58

Acknowledgments & Gratitude

First & Foremost, Praise and Gratitude to Our Father God-Allah.

Honors to His Noble Prophet Drew Ali for bringing back to us our Nationality & Ancient & Divine Creed: That we may Learn to Love Instead of Hate;

Honors to the Forerunner, President Marcus Mosiah Garvey II for preparing the way for our Prophet;

To the Sisters that first helped propagate Unity & Sisterhood in North America under the tenants of Islam;

To Sister Augustus Bey who, with the assistance of her husband & Temple, first made this information available;

To Sister Clara Muhammad who's tireless work played in integral part in the establishment of the Nation of Islam & the M.G.T., which to this day puts into practice the instructions contained herein;

To Clara Muhammad School & Muslim Mosque #2, Chicago, who helped & guided me during my short though memorable stint in their M.G.T.;

To the Moorish Sisters of California who's desire for this information encouraged me

To those who tried to discourage me, for it is only through adversity that a warrior learns her strength.

To the Muslim/ Moslem she-ros in history who's stories remind me of what real adversity can be & how it can be overcome though Islam.

Peace & Love to You All

Preface

Excerpt from the Moorish Guide Newspaper announcing establishment of the Moorish National Sisters' Auxiliary

---

MOORISH GUIDE
NATIONAL EDITION

VOL. 1 NO. 13   FRIDAY FEB.5, 1929   PRICE 10 CENTS

PROPHET BEGINS SECOND TOUR

THE MOORISH NATIONAL AUXILIARY WELL ON WAY
SISTERS' AUXILIARY

The Moorish National Sisters' Auxiliary was organized December 17, 1928 with a small membership of ten members. The membership has grown in two months to the enrollment of twenty-seven faithful, dutiful Moorish Sisters. Their paramont object is to uplift fallen humanity and be the right hand of the Prophet by their kind words, works and deeds. They have so soon sustained a "Necessity Fund" to help a sister or brother in distress and care for the sick, poor and needy.

The headquarters are at Unity Hall, 2nd floor
No Joining Fees. Monthly dues 25 cents

TO HOLD TAG DAY WITHIN TEMPLE NUMBER ONE

The first Moorish National Tag Day will be celebrated by Temple No.1 of Chicago, from March 17-29. The tags will be sold within the temples prior to and after each meeting held between the above dates. The nominal price will be ten cents. All subordinate temples will receive a sample tag so that the idea may be passed along to them for their consideration. The tag will be held under the auspices of the Moorish National Sisters' Auxiliary.

There will be a week of sacrifice. This will be celebrated a week before the return of the Prophet from his tour around the temples. For the whole week members will drop as much money as they can spare into a box. Upon his return the box will be presented to him for fallen humanity.

Sis.Levine El, President   Sis.Lloydd Bey, Vice President
Sis.Rhodes El, Recording Sec.   Sis.M.Drew Ali, Financial Sec.,Treasurer
Sis.Adams El,Chrm.Necessity Fund Sis.Shaw El, Chaplain

MEANING OF TAG
Quote of PROPHET NOBLE DREW ALI by Bro.J.Blakely-Bey, Past S.G.A.M.

The HEART means love, dear to the next person or just plain goodness to all mankind. The color GREEN means "LIFE EVERLASTING". In the center of the heart is a five pointed GREEN STAR pointed at the word UNICE which means " PEACE and UNITY AMONG MOORISH-AMERICANS."

Editor's Note
How to use this guide.

So that you may make most effective use of the instructions contained in this guide, I encourage the reader to have close at hand the following:

- A good standard dictionary of the English language, preferably one printed before 1965. The reason for this suggestion are two-fold: First, the book you hold is revised from a text originally published in 1928. Some of the words contained herein may no longer be in common use and/ or may have a different definition in modern dictionaries. Second, I suggest using a dictionary of this sort as many definitions—especially those pertaining to our people—were altered after the Civil Rights Movement in the United States. An example would be comparing the definitions of "American" in a pre-1965 dictionary versus one printed more recently.

  - Please note, there is no glossary contained in this guide to encourage use of a dictionary. Man—nor woman— knows not by being told.

- A Holy Quran of Mecca. The Prophet Noble Drew Ali did not release the Holy Koran of the Moorish Science Temple of America Circle Seven until between 1926 and 1928. The Moorish Holy Temple of Science, predecessor of the Moorish Science Temple of America, was founded in 1913 (Key 9). One must therefore ask themselves, what was the Prophet teaching from prior to the release of the Circle 7? The use of the Holy Quran of Mecca is further validated by its reference on our M.S.T. of A. Nationality Card: *"I do hereby declare that you are a Moslem under the divine Laws of the Holy Koran of Mecca..."*

- Holy Koran of the Moorish Science Temple of America Circle Seven

- A bible of your choice.

As you read this guide you will notice spaces to the exterior of the pages. These are reserved for any notes you may wish to make. Scholarly works encourage the student to make notes next to the item being noted for quick future reference.

Willing you much success in your endeavor to improve yourself, and thereby, our Nation,

Peace & Love

Sis. Tauheedah S. Najee-Ullah El

Introduction

Our class of womanhood teaches those attributes and character traits of Allah that distinguishes us as Women and Sisters in Auxiliary. We are uplifted and perfected with these national standards which make us holy, and make our nation free. We are a National and Divine Religious Society, truly the Mothers of Civilization.

The meaning of Sisters in Auxiliary is that they are the same righteous of the Prophet Noble Drew Ali in all necessities. This is the name of the teaching of gifted women in America. How to sew, cook, keep home. How to take care of our husbands and rear our children in truth. How to act National and Divine and be ourselves.

We are being seeded with the civilization of tomorrow. We have to prepare them for that future so we must live the life that Allah wants us to live. So Eat to Live!

There is but one Prophet over any and every nation. He lives and dies, and another takes his place who is just like him, there is no difference. Just know that Allah is man. You though are Allah in person. I just want you to understand that, but you must be taught that. You must know about the devil and his cares of the world. Allah in man will grant life to you when you obey him. Forsake all who forsake Allah in man, friend or foe, family or foreigner. You cannot be a member of this class if you don't live the laws of Allah.

Proclaim our Moorish Divine Creed and American Nationality and be yourselves.

Learn to be at peace in your home, don't be lazy. If your home is nasty it can't be peaceful. First learn to make your home heaven. A righteous woman is pleasing to a man for a wife. The square inch often spoken of means, we must be square in righteousness before leaving this earth home. Twelve inches equals one foot. Twelve tribes equals the Earth's inhabitants of Nations. A square foot equals 14.4 inches, which is 12" by 12". Then if it takes 12" by 12" inches to make only one square foot or 14.4 inches, then this teaches us that to be able to stand on the square of righteousness, one must pass the test of the twelve tribes. The same as 12 x 12 equals 144. Then we are square 144,000 righteous people, ready to become a cube. A cube is a solid of six equal sides or faces, thus known as equality. Where there are no decent women, there are no decent men. The Sisters in Auxiliary must help and strive hard to uplift the virtue of intelligence in our Moorish American Nation.

Indecent acts such as enchanting looks, shaking, and seducing men. If a lovely man incites in you indecent thoughts, you should look away from him and lower your gaze, for he incites the lower self.

Cover yourself, for when you tempt men to bad thoughts, it makes the man have like desire in his heart. This desire is not easy to conquer. Our ancestors and Sisters in the East show no forms, wear sheets of clothes and wrap up. Righteous women everywhere robe themselves, so that they may be known and respected.

Holy Quran Ch. 33: 31, 32, 33, 36.
H.K. M.S.T.A. 21

The Moslem Girls' Training & General Civilization Class

Instruction On The Law of Women in Islam

The Almighty Allah, The Lord of the Worlds has sent down to us a Prophet to save and deliver us from our enemies who have robbed our people in the wilderness of "North America" completely of the knowledge of themselves and anyone else, and keep them in a state of fear and sorrow, hunger, nakedness and away from salvation. Deprived of Freedom, Justice, and Equality, our colonizers kill them at his will. Make and teach us to do everything but righteousness and keep us sick, blind, deaf and dumb, by teaching us to eat the wrong food.

So our Prophet Himself has called us into this Auxiliary to reform us from the unrighteousness and uncleanliness of this devil's wicked and adulterous generation. That Allah sit us in heaven at once and destroy those who have destroyed us and to reform us. This means that you must be willing to forsake the ways and teachings of the colonizers and accept the teachings of our own leaders, from the mouth of Almighty God through his Prophet, Noble Drew Ali.

The end of the colonized world has come and Allah (to whom be praise in both heaven and on earth) is ready to destroy this world, and bring in a completely new world and a new people out of us who are not dead and corrupted from the enslavement of the sin. A Moslem is a being who is entirely in tune with the will of Allah. The Moslems are pleased with Allah, and Allah pleased with the Moslems. We have not set our will but by the breath of Allah, and Allah rewards the Moslems with Peace and Love, grants to us out of His understanding, wisdom, knowledge, food, clothing, shelter, transportation, nationality and divine creed, and thus protects us against harm. Allah fights all their battles and brings their enemies to their knees in submission, and makes them Muslims.

A Moslem is a holy person, practicing all that is divine and natural, and instructs everyone that does that not love and obey Allah and His Prophets. Whether it be their fathers, and mothers, brothers and sisters, husbands or wives or their children. They make believers of these people that do not believe in Allah and

His Prophets. A Moslem will not try to imitate foreigners in anything except their good words, works and deeds.

The present world is full of hatred, slander, lewdness, murder theft and everything that harms. They have taken the world for sport and play. Truth and justice is trodden under foot. Therefore Allah has promised to destroy such an evil and unrighteous nation from the face of the Earth and offer to us chance to live if we would only forsake the present enemies of unrighteousness. The Moslem woman is civilized and is not an ignorant savage. Her intelligence is the purest and noblest of all. Her home is a place of love and contentment, her husband is happy with her. Her children are taught righteousness from the cradle. She wastes not her time away into idleness. The following ethics must be followed by all that accept Islam and enter into this Sister's Auxiliary class:

1. Clean internal and external at all times.
2. Do not use tobacco in any form or snuff.
3. Drink no alcoholic beverage (intoxicating drink).
4. You shall not tempt men with your beauty in any form, by displaying nude parts of your body, hair, legs, backs and hips, singing love songs, enchanting looks, walking, sitting, or lying down.
5. You shall not wear tight form fitting clothes in public, nor low neck garments that show your chest or breast. Wear no high heeled shoes and go not bear legged in public during any season of the year.
6. You should not use makeup when going in public, such as paints and long nails. Do use hot irons on your hair, European-made greases, or so-called hair tonics. Stay away from European places of amusement.
7. You should wear an over garment in the Moorish Science Temple of America that you may be known. Also, wear a head covering, preferably your turban with crescent pin.
8. You should eat such foods as Allah has commanded and taught us to eat. Adults in good health should not eat more than two meals per day, and children in good health should not eat over three. Touch not the animal flesh.
9. Commit not adultery. Go not near to it.

10. Kill not your children to cover your own shame of adultery. Nor for fear of hunger destroy the seed of your womb.

11. The students in the S.A. Shall be trained into the knowledge of general housekeeping, how to cook, sew, clean house, read, write, and speak clearly.

12. You should not marry non-Moslems. A righteous Moslem cannot love one who says they love you but does not love Allah and your religion; Islamism.

13. You shall not gaze upon beautiful men lest they turn your heart into unclean thoughts. Cast down your gaze and look not upon them. Nor listen to their love songs or any other sign of enchantment.

14. You shall keep up fasting for fasting keeps you from evil and gives your good health. If you want to marry and cannot find a husband of your choice, then keep chaste until Allah gives you one. Allah knows what you keep secret and what you manifest. Keep up prayer and give charity.

15. Obey Allah and his Prophet.

Sisters in Auxiliary

The Sisters in Auxiliary are Moorish Women of America and the world whose divine instruction has been uplifted by the soul attributes of the Prophet Noble Drew Ali, Allah's Prophet. The Sisters in Auxiliary are Noble women who have redeemed themselves from being a slave to sin.

In Auxiliary, sisters find all the answers to life's questions concerning Noble women. The Sisters in Auxiliary are the rocks of their family, pillars of their communities, and foundations for the nation. When a sister enters the Auxiliary, she is given order to control the chaos that is called life through the Divine Guidance and National Leadership of our Prophet, Noble Drew Ali. Immediately and continually, the Sisters in Auxiliary go through the process of being uplifted, redeemed and perfected. Praise Allah for divinely preparing the Prophet of Ali, whom we give highest honor, to redeem his people from their sinful ways.

The Sisters in Auxiliary under the Divine Guidance of the Prophet, Noble Drew Ali, are starting to work toward perfection. We as a nation of people cannot be civilized acting like foreign savages. The church and Christianity cannot truly offer the Moorish American redemption or salvation.

The Moorish Americans, who go and have gone to the highest schools of learning must still proclaim and practice their National and Divine Creed.

The dictionary gives us only one definition for nationality. True Nationality unveils the disguises of second class citizenship.

We must work, in thought, words and deeds, to become perfected and of the noblest character. We have to be taught by the Prophet of Ali what "noble" is, in order for us to become noble and acquire all the highest soul attributes.

The most simplest but hardest custom in the highest plane of life for the unconscious sister is controlling her tongue--or mouth--as it is commonly put.

Sisters in Auxiliary do not gossip, slander, speak loud or vulgar language. This is the law and the law must live. We have to enforce the law in order to save the nation. Sisters hold tight to your salvation and unity. Work toward acquiring the highest dignity by closing your mouth and opening your mind, eyes, ears and heart, and by putting your able hands to work in your home maintaining, caring for and maintaining your husband and family. All Sisters must learn the truth and the divine truth and serve as the example to their children daily.

The Prophet of Ali teaches us that the Sisters in Auxiliary, must learn to partake only in divine and national conversations. Study constantly so as to be able to properly proclaim and practice your national and divine creed as given to you by your Prophet of Ali who was divinely prepared by Allah, the Great God.

The Nationalizing of a People

One of the many programs of the Divine Mission of the Prophet of Ali, Allah's Prophet

We rise giving all perfect praise to Allah the Great God. We give highest honors to His Prophet, Noble Drew Ali and the Moorish Divine and National Movement of North America.

The Divine Movement of the Last Prophet in these days, Noble Drew Ali is the governance of our Moorish American vast estate under trusteeship of the Moorish Science temple of America. Our purpose is to uplift fallen humanity through the very comprehensive Divine Plan of the Ages. We need to learn more about the Divine Movement of the Prophet of Ali, and the marvelous burden it carries, then we will appreciate, honor, respect and give thanks to Allah for preparing and ordaining His Divine Prophet of Ali.

As you learn of the Holiness of the Prophet of Ali, you will also learn of your own holiness and the divine love Allah has to give you. We will also learn of the National love which Prophet Ali had for his people while he performed his duty for Allah, the Nationalizing of the Moorish people of America.

We, the Moorish Americans, know that we are in the right place, at the right time for the right reason.

A Few Good Moors

We are uplifting into a new world of salvation and unity. As we look forward to entering heaven or earth we are reminded of the need for qualified missionaries of Islam in America.

As we expected, the Movement is, and probably will continue to be besieged by propaganda of the most vicious kind to attempt to cause a shadow over our pure light.

As Moslems, we simply ignore the malicious attempt of falsehood manifest to destroy and defame our organization, we will forever be strong enough in our efforts to build this Divine Nation under the leadership of Prophet and Guidance of Allah.

With the Sisters Circle of Islam, we must strengthen our bonds to be able and worthy of the holy blessing we are given the opportunity to receive. Highly qualified people the world over are literally begging for jobs working for the Prophet of Ali.

The judgment is now on!

NOBLE DREW ALI, Founder of
The Moorish Science Temple of America

How to Dress

This is a warning the S.A. To adopt Moorish Dress and hair styles and seek to marry a traditional Moorish Brother.

No style of dress is to be worn but the style of the real Moorish people. This is the way we dress!

The head piece of the traditional and tribal Moorish people are best for the Believers of Islamism.

If you are not satisfied with your own free national styles then you are a slave to sin.

Matt. 26:42
Holy Qur'an 7:27
Study the Book of Ruth

- The robe of the righteousness is white.
- We wear Moorish slippers and never wear out our shoes.
- We never go out of our homes without the proper head covering.
- We may wear a 'natural,' braided hairstyles and locs/dredlocs only. No perms, presses or dyes!!
- We strive always to be ourselves and practice our national and divine creed.
- We should not wear more than three colors at a time.
- We wear conservative clothes. We wear all the colors of the rainbow.
- We always have our clothes neatly pressed and immaculately clean. Shoes must be shined and properly soled. Pocket books will be clean and shined with any papers in order.
- Our nails should be trimmed and clean.
- We do not wear hanging earrings outside the home.
- Our hair should be clean, combed and well groomed.
- Our teeth should be given daily care in the form of brushing and bi-annual visits to a dentist.

- We make sure the day before we wear a garment, that it is properly mended where mending is needed.
- We must have our garments tailored. It is undignified to wear a garment that does not fit or is made improperly.
- We must strive to look clean, neat, well-pressed, and well-tailored each and every day, not just on special occasions. When we appear in public, they (the public) do not look at us merely as individuals, they see us as missionaries of the Prophet Drew Ali and the Moorish Nation. You will hear them say daily, "There is one of those Moorish sisters. You, know, the Prophet's followers!" As Moorish sisters, we must give a good impression of Islamism and our leader and teacher whenever we leave our homes.
- We must remove spots and soil from our garments, and regularly check our hemlines and necklines to ensure they are in good condition.

Laws and Instructions

"The Restrictive Law is our success!"

Moslem Rules

1. A Moslem must show the greatest intelligence at all times.
2. Never be the aggressor by words or actions. In the event you are attacked, stick together in battle as a solid wall.
3. Obey the laws of the land or government you live under for if you cannot keep these laws, how can you obey the laws of Allah? However, if these laws conflict with the laws of Allah, then fear Allah, for Allah alone you must fear.
4. What is the duty of the Grand Sheik, Assistant Grand Sheik and other Sheiks? The G.S.'s duty is to give the orders to the Assistant G.S. The Assistant G.S.'s duty is to teach the members and train them.
5. A Moslem's word is bond, and bond is life. I will give my life before my word shall fail.
6. Moslems must always keep purity of mind and cleanliness of body.
7. Moslems do not give or use oaths.
8. A Moslem acknowledges and recognizes that he is a member of the Moorish Nations and act accordingly in the name of Allah. As Moslems, we must set the example for the New Believers.
9. We must recognize the necessity for unity and group operation.
10. Stop needless criticisms of your brother or sister. We must remember that jealousy destroys from within.
11. The Law of Islamism says that if one sister has a bowl of soup, the other sister has half of that bowl; her success is your success.
12. Be patient in matters where others are involved. Remember: there were times when we that know, knew not.
13. Do not take the bad side of a thing that appears to us as bad. There is always a good side, it is better to take that side.

14. Actions are judged by the intentions. Actions may appear wrong, but motives bring rewards.
15. Seek not to find fault in your sister or brother. This does not mean making unnecessary excuses for wrongdoing.
16. Only by true repentance and reform can we escape the consequence of our errors.
17. If you should see a Member in error, correct them in the strictest privacy.
18. There should be at least two witnesses in order to bring a charge against a sister or brother.
19. Do not pray as a Moslem and act otherwise.
20. Moslems should not participate in activities leading away from Allah.
21. A true Moslem should act justly not only to other Moslems, but also non-Moslems and even those who are enemies of Islam.

    "I, the G.S. must be cared for, also Secretary and Business Manager, but these must work hard to attract New Believers. Fear not about your bread."

On violation of the following Laws, you are subject to dismissal from the Temple for no less than 30 days:

1. Sleeping in the Temple.
2. Keeping late hours.
3. Using narcotics (dope, heroin).
4. Married and taking up time with other sisters.
5. Socializing with non-Believers.
6. Drunkenness.
7. Unclean homes.
8. Personal hygiene.
9. Watching the movement of the opposite sex.
10. Lying or stealing from one another.
11. Gambling.
12. Eating pork.
13. Gossiping on one another.

Orders of the Sisters in Auxiliary

A) The Secretary should have all the Artifacts set for presentation before the Grand Sheik arrives. Let it remain until the meeting is dismissed.

B) The Moslems must be 100% clean and loving to one another. Their clothes and their homes must be clean at all times. Do not let Dirty Moors into the Temple.

C) The Investigator must investigate or visit homes unexpectedly once per week.

D) We must see to it that the Temple is kept clean of filth at all times. Only clean floors, clean walls, and clean seats must exist in the Temple.

E) If a Moslem says that he is with us and associates with our enemies, they are a lie and we must stay away from them.

F) Hurry! Hurry! Hurry! Lose no more time, have no more quarreling among the faithful. The Law settles all arguments. Get after the Believers! Put them to work and all that come must be willing to help by giving all he or she can to the cause of Islam.

G) Cast out all rotten apples, quick. Keep your ears and eyes open to those smart crooked deceivers who will always try to put one over. Have all searched 100% before entering the Temple. Make the Moslems comb their hair, keep their clothes cleaned and pressed, their shoes shined, hair trimmed. If they do not clean up, they are out of luck with us.

H) Make all sisters and girls join the Adept Class and train them fast. Make them brave members and willing at any time to give their life for Allah's sake and righteousness.

Proper Attitude

When speaking of she who is kind, one speaks of she who is most loved and chosen for Himself (Allah). She is a child among children, born of the holy of holies.

For when in the presence of someone who is kind, one feels soothed and elevated by them. By kindness I do not mean an individual who allows any and every passerby to misuse and abuse her, but rather by kindness that individual sees in the person she encounters. The essence of their God-like selves and the essence of herself. With this insight she intuitively reaches out and touches, loves and soothes that person's spirit, heart and soul. Thereby, both the person who is kind and the person who received the kindness is each elevated to higher spiritual plateaus within their individual realms. For Kindness is an Attribute of Allah!

When speaking of a sister, we say her complete name. If the Grand Sheik gives someone a holy name then use it. Call her by her holy name. It is said that Sister Drew Ali desired to be called by her full name; Sister Drew Ali.

We should always be courteous to our husband. Saying please, thank you, and yes sir.

When we enter the room, we give the greetings. The responsibility lies with you to extend the greeting first. Give the greetings to all present (as a group).

We should speak only loud enough for the person we are speaking with to hear us.

When using the rest room, leave it clean and neat; leave no soiled things nor personal objects behind.

When wearing our garments, we should not go in a store or restaurant to purchase candy, ice cream, or the like.

It is better to send a brother to the store for you.

When going on a trip, you should carry something with you to eat.

We do not stay in motels alone with traveling abroad unescorted.

We should strive to shop with a sister for there is safety in numbers.

When shopping, know what you are buying, get it, and move quickly to your next destination.

When someone visits your home, have adequate clean articles for each person and a place to dispose of soiled towels.

Language

- A foolish woman is clamorous. She is simple and knoweth nothing.
- " So I said I will take heed to my ways that I sin not with my tongue."
- We in the M.S.T. Must strive to speak calmly, softly and distinctively. Our words should be carefully chosen and spoken in quiet tones (think five times before speaking).
- Do not be snappy with others regardless of how you feel. It shows weakness and lack of self-control. Boisterous, loud voices are a sign of vulgarity and shows a lack of refinement. We do not laugh loud, but rather softly. Do not belittle others or laugh when they have made an error. Do not laugh when you have made an error, as it shows a lack of understanding on your part. It is also rude.
- Do not become loud and boisterous when being corrected for an error you have made, rather take the correction calmly, intelligently and gracefully as this is a civilized attitude.
- When making suggestions, to anyone, keep them in the form and tone of suggestions and do not make them sound like orders, as we are not to give orders, but to take them.
- When in public, we keep our voices low and use proper words to express ourselves. This applies also when in the presence of brothers: speak softly to them, not loud or noisily.
- Avoid anger as it tends to make you lose control and possibly say things for which you may later be sorry. Anger brings out the worst in you. This is a negative emotion and it shows lack of self-control.

- "And in their mouth was found no guile for they were without fault before the throne of God."
- When in public, we keep our voices low and use proper words to express ourselves. This applies also when in the presence of brothers: speak softly to them, not loud or noisily.
- Avoid anger as it tends to make you lose control and possibly say things for which you may later be sorry. Anger brings out the worst in you. This is a negative emotion and it shows lack of self-control.
- "And in their mouth was found no guile for they were without fault before the throne of God."

Conversation

The art of conversation is a simple matter of good manners which are easy to describe and even easier to carry out. All general conversation, whether at the level of a great art or a little pleasure, should be conducted within this Act of Civilized Limits:

1.   No monologues. An informative speech, no matter how interesting, cannot be considered conversation.

2.   No language which all in the group do not understand.

3.   No member of the group should be left out. The one who is speaking should always look from one to the other. No topic too difficult for any member of the group should be discussed.

4.   Sometimes in a group of well informed people, there will be one who though joining happily in the conversation, is obviously beyond their depths. In cases like this, steer the conversation to another subject.

5.   No blanket or harsh attacks on religion, nationalist, political parties, etc.

Some facts about "GOSSIP"

1. What is easy to say may be hard to bear.
2. What you don't see with your eyes, don't invent with your mouth.
3. It is easier to hear a secret than to keep it.
4. A tongue can be a dangerous weapon.
5. If you want to find out what's happening in your house, talk to your neighbors.
6. Loose tongues are worse than wicked hands.
7. Our ears often don't hear what our mouths say.
8. Run from gossip as you would from Danger.
9. Gossip is the most common of human habits and cause of the most trouble.
10. People eat and drink together, yet pierce each other.
11. Your friend has a friend, and your friend's friend has as friend (so be discreet).
12. From a man's mouth you can tell what he is.
13. Gossip: Nature's telephone.
14. The whisperer separates friends.

"Study, read and keep up with the news so you may have something to talk about."

How NOT to Use Our Tongues

"When you open your mouth, people can see into your mind."

1. Do not rail or brawl against anyone.
2. Do not speak evil of others in their absence.
3. Do not exaggerate in any of your statements.
4. Do not speak harshly, or make fun of the less fortunate.
5. Do not swear, lie, or indulge in impure language.
6. Do not make random and improper assertions.
7. Do not speak harshly or violently.
8. Do not deceive people by circulating false reports.
9. Do not offer lip service.
10. Do not use Allah's name falsely or in vain.

How We SHOULD Use Our Tongues

"When you open your mouth, people can see into your mind."

1. To convey useful information to our people. (Convey good news and do good deeds and they shall have gardens wherein rivers flow with great rewards.)
2. To speak kindly of each other.
3. To be truthful and simple in our statements.
4. To comfort and console the fearful.
5. To cheer the timid and fearful.
6. To defend the innocent and oppressed.
7. To reprove and admonish the wicked.
8. To congratulate the success of the virtuous.
9. To confess faults to one another.
10. o pray and seek the praise of our God Allah.

Posture

We never sit with our legs crossed as this is bad for health and very unrefined.

We do not fold our arms in front.

We do not slouch when sitting or standing.

We always sit with spine straight.

We do not bite our fingernails.

We do not lean head on arms or hands as we are not alert when doing this.

We never switch, stroll, or bob up and down when walking.

We walk erect with shoulders pulled back, buttocks tucked in, slightly tilted, forward moving quickly, quietly, gracefully, and with dignity.

We always stand on two feet.

We never put hands on hips.

We try to keep our hands away from our face, hair or headpiece (when wearing).

When walking up or down stairs, we gently lift the hem of our garment.

When standing, we have hands gently at our sides.

When sitting, make sure the fold of your skirt is completely over as not to show the legs.

When sitting, keep both legs together as it looks more dignified.

When sitting, fold hands in lap.

All of your body positions and movements should reflect your finest qualities and highest morals in a way that demands respect from everyone. This is civilized.

"Reprove not a scorner, lest he hate thee; rebuke a wise man, and he will love thee."

Mannerism

After finishing her studies as a student of the M.G.T., the Moslem sister is never again seen wearing vulgar, immodest, indecent attire. All of her body positions and movements reflect her finest qualities, highest morals, and in a way that demands respect of everyone, Moor or otherwise, Moslem or non-Moslem. Her words are carefully chosen and spoken in tones that reflect the finest qualities of the Moslem woman, for she is taught that Allah hates boisterous, loud or rough voices. According to the Holy Qur'an, "...these bad characteristics greatly detract from the delicate, soft, feminine beauty which is the very nature of the Moorish Woman.

Manners

Etiquette is a set of rules for proper conduct, observed by polite society the world over. The essence of etiquette is kindness and consideration for the other person. Conventions change along with the times but the basic rules of good manners never change.

Good behavior is everybody's business and good taste can be everyone's goal. A code of behavior is an inevitable part of life in any community. A system or set of rules is vital for anything in which human beings are involved. Common sense demands a system. The value of etiquette can be analyzed as follows:

1. It has a practical value because it has made time- and thought-saving by addressing technicalities, such as wording and form of invitation.
2. It has an attractive side like putting flowers on the table for the sake of beauty and gracefulness.
3. It has a great civic value—this is the prime contribution of etiquette. Civil value lies in the fact that etiquette imposes consideration of others.
4. It demands willingness to discipline oneself for the sake of others.
5. Etiquette has sometimes been questioned because it can be it can be used as a substitute for kindness or gratitude. But the one who pretends to a virtue and lacks it is not as dangerous to society as the one who convinces others that virtue is unnecessary.

6. The greatest value of etiquette is its value to the individual. Good behavior may be useful to society, but it is part of man. "Manners make the man." It is part of your character and you cannot escape it or leave it behind.

7. Good manners in public are perhaps more than anything else the mark of a civilized people. Without them, what should be perfectly normal action, like sitting on the bus or waiting in line for a ticket can be turned into a maddening experience.

8. A Moslem sister is never loud and she speaks in a soft voice, especially in public. We are taught by the Prophet Drew Ali that the Moorish mother is the key to all humanity.

9. Let us attract our lost sisters with our dress and our manners.

10. When we lower our dignity with loose expression and vulgarity of words, it lowers us.

11. Display our best nature, conduct, accomplishment, smiles and appearances at home as well as abroad.

12. We do not shake hands with our gloves on, nor do with pray with gloves on.

13. A Moslem sister would never eat walking down the street, nor would she go into a store to buy a piece of candy. She would send a brother for her.

14. An attitude of deference and respect whenever anyone enters the Temple should be taught to Moorish children at the earliest possible age. The proper behavior ought to be observed by the young from the attitude and behavior of their seniors.

15. When you get up in the morning, dress yourself properly, you never know who may come to visit. Take care of yourself first.

16. When in the presence of the Grand Sheik, never speak louder than our Grand Sheik. When entering his home, always show respect for his home. When entering any Moslem's home, always show respect for their home.

"I will praise thee for I am fearfully and wonderfully made: marvelous are thy works. For who can find a virtuous woman? For her price is far above rubies. Strength and honor are her clothing: and she shall rejoice in time to come. She opens her mouth with wisdoms and in her tongue is the law of kindness. Many daughters have done virtuously, but thou excellest them all. For favor is deceitful and beauty is vain.

But a sister that feareth Allah, she shall be praised. Give her of the fruits of her hands: and let her own works praise her in the gates."

The Dangers of Being Overweight

The problem of overweight is studied in the Sister's Auxiliary; a class set up by Prophet Drew Ali. We learn that most of the bodily ailments are directly or indirectly traceable to overweight. It is no exaggeration to say that the fat die young. You seldom see a fat person over 60 years old. We should seriously consider the subject of overweight if we wish to live happy and useful lives. An excess of fat causes the individual to become INACTIVE. That inactivity in turn causes a multitude of problems. As you may have noticed, the fat woman is inclined to be lazy. She likes to sit and take things easy. She does not like activity and because she is not active, she gets fatter. The fatter she gets, the less inclined she is to be active. She soon finds herself in a vicious circle – she gets fatter and fatter and at the same time becomes lazier and lazier.

Dangers of Inactivity

A direct result of this inactivity is CONSTIPATION, because a certain amount of exercise is necessary for the normal functioning of the organs or elimination. Constipation causes "auto-intoxication" or self poisoning. This results from the accumulation of decayed matter in the large intestine. This poison is absorbed by the bloodstream and carried to all parts of the body, producing headaches, bad breath, sluggishness and skin deformities, such as blotches, pimples, and even the appearance of premature old age. Now this same inactivity is a predisposing cause of diabetes; a disease characterized by the inability of the body to utilize sugar. It is a known fact that seven out of every ten people who develop diabetes are overweight. During exercise, the muscles burn up large amounts of sugar. The fat sister does not exercise her muscles enough, and hence, and excess amount of sugar is accumulated in her body. Moreover, she dearly likes her sweets and almost always overeats. Thus, she takes in more sugar than her body needs or muscles use. And she then lays the foundation for the dreaded disease. Diabetes is curable only by reversing these bad habits. Sister, stop digging your own grave with your knife and fork!

Overweight Develops Heart Trouble

But the overweight are quite likely to develop heart trouble . My dear sister, do you have a shortness of breath and a palpitation in the heart? If you do, you may have what is known as fatty heart. It means that the normal action of the muscles of your heart are being embarrassed by the presence of fatty tissue. You should not impose on your heart because it has a pretty big job to perform anyway: Remember, it must beat continuously from the moment of birth to the end of life. Why then do you burden it with unnecessary eating?

Do you have terrible headaches and dizzy spells? If you do, you may suspect HIGH BLOOD PRESSURE, a condition caused by overeating of food rich in proteins, such as fresh meats and eggs. When you develop high blood pressure, you may be sure that you have just about eaten yourself to death. You must pay the supreme penalty for living other than yourself. There are many other diseases, for instance cancer and Bright's disease, which seem to follow the overweight and eventually overtake them. Of course you know that the overweight person does not have such a good chance of recovering from pneumonia. Also in passing, it may be well to drop the hint that the overweight sister loses the right and privilege of motherhood at a much younger age than her more slender friend. In closing it should be said that the overweight person is not only physically inactive, but mentally slow. The Moslem knows that the overweight person is the good natured individual who does not care to be disturbed. She does not care to exercise her mental faculties. She would rather sleep. Her whole system is poisoned and her brain cells cannot function properly. Islamism does not tolerate anything the destroys the health or impairs the intellect. Therefore Moslems, watch the scales.

Some Great Tips on Caring For Our Hair

- Section the hair and plait it before going to bed. This will almost completely rid you of tangles the next morning.
- Sleep with a satin scarf on your head or with a satin pillowcase. This helps to stop split ends by minimizing the friction between your head and the pillow.
- While conditioning your hair, gently comb it out with a de-tangling comb. This gets rid of a lot of tangles.
- Oil the scalp, not the hair. Follow with gently brushing the hair away from the scalp to distribute the oil to your hair.
- Don't use petroleum or mineral oil based products on the hair or scalp. They attract dust and don't really penetrate.
- Always use a leave in conditioner.
- You should wash your hair no more than once a week or every ten days. This will prevent your hair drying out.
- After a workout at the gym, rinse your hair thoroughly with warm water to remove salt as this can by drying.
- Moorish women should steer clear of any hair products that contains alcohol. These can be drying. Also avoid balsam as it does not contain the type of moisturizing we need.
- Never use a boar bristle brush!! Boar is another name for hog!!

Tips on Combing and Brushing the Hair

Brushing:
Dampen the brush bristles with a little warm water before applying it to the hair. This helps to soften the hair while brushing. A soft, baby brush will further prevent hair lost during brushing

Combing:
Combs are good for combing long hair or creating parts for braiding or twisting. Try not to use it when the hair is completely wet or completely dry. This can cause the hair to break. You should have

completely dry. This can cause the hair to break. You should have a large-toothed comb for combing and a small one for parting. Separate hair into four sections, then comb it section by section.

Picking:
The pick is probably one of the most recognized symbols in natural hair care. The pick is the natural hair's best friend. Picks can be used for just about any natural style. It's a great way to detangle the hair. Before picking out your hair, dampen the hair with a small amount of water or leave-in conditioner. This will help loosen up the tangles. Be sure to work conditioner into the ends of the hair.

Oiling:
The most effective natural treatment for dry hair is hot oil. Warm olive oil in a saucepan. Using a cotton ball, dab the warmed oil on the scalp and roots of the hair. Wrap your oiled hair in a hot towel and let it sit for 20-30 minutes. Wash hair thoroughly. For added moisture add 3 tablespoons of plain yogurt mixed with an egg, then follow the above instructions.

"Make it Yourself" Moorish Hair Care Products

Avocados make great moisturizers!

Mash the pulp of an avocado and add a teaspoon of olive oil to it. Prior to shampooing, section hair and apply mixture to the roots and ends of the hair. Cover your hair with a plastic cap and sit under a dryer. The dryer will help the oils penetrate.

Mayonnaise is one of the best deep conditioners you can find!

Lightly apply the mayonnaise to the hair and scalp, cover your hair with a plastic cap then sit under a dryer, or wrap the head in a hot towel, then let it sit for 15-20 minutes. Thoroughly wash the hair until the mayonnaise is completely gone.

M.oslem Girls' Training & Sisters' Auxiliary
Students Class Creed

1. We will strive to control our attentions in order to do a careful and accurate job on our requirements.
2. I will strive to improve my listening skills, take notes, read and think of what is being said and fit it into what I already know.
3. I will strive to review what is taught and keep and overall pattern in mind.
4. I will strive to improve my handwriting through practice because I need ease in handwriting to transfer my thoughts to paper.
5. I will strive to keep a record of assignments and keep homework up to date.
6. I will strive to give a new sister a good impression of Islamism as I realize this is important to help her revive her hidden qualities.
7. I will strive to have a complete notebook and keep it up to date.
8. I will strive to dress and act like the kind of Moslem I wish to become.
9. I will strive to follow instructions, asking questions when I don't understand.
10. We will strive each day to do something to help the Program.

Ways and Reasons to be Successful on the Job:

1. Apply for the job as a member of the M.S.T. of A.
2. Dress in accordance with the Temple's instructions.
3. Conduct yourself in a business-like manner while maintaining a cautious pleasantness.
4. Never encourage small talk conversations or become interested in gossip and be spared of them.
5. Give full-time and satisfactory work.
6. Be not ashamed of practicing what the M.S.T. of A. instructs and carry yourself in a manner reflecting what the Holy Koran teaches as not to misrepresent our people.

Do these things because of facts presenting themselves daily which are: Allah is god. The European's time of rule is over, and the first physical man is the Asiatic man.

You need a teacher to teach you, and only the Prophet Noble Drew Ali, the Prophet of Allah, has the Divine Instructions to teach the Moorish American woman how to become more civilized and respected. Come to the Prophet's Temple and accept and follow the Greatest Man you know as your Prophet.

100 Do's and Don'ts of the Moslem Girls' Training & Sisters' Auxiliary

1. Your head is to be covered at all times (in public), especially during meeting times.
2. Your arms are to be covered at least 1 ½ inches below the elbow.
3. Your dress is to be at a proper length at all times (in public). Children should be in pantaloons and ankle length skirts or jumper tops.
4. No tight fitting or revealing garments in public.
5. Your shoes should be no higher than one inch. No cut outs.
6. The neckline is to be properly closed. There are many ways to do this.
7. You should not cross your legs (over knee), except down at the ankles. This was first done by the Caucasian to show off the curvature of the thighs. It is also bad for your circulation. Your legs should always be properly closed.
8. No fingernail polish is to be worn except for the clear nail hardener. We should also keep up with our nail care.
9. NO MAKE UP is to be worn. Let your natural beauty shine through. No relaxing, coloring, or frying.
10. Do not eat in public, while riding public transportation, or while walking down the street.
11. Do not yell across or down the street, nor out of car or house windows. ALLAH DOES NOT LIKE LOUD BOISTEROUS WOMEN.

12. Bathe at least once a day. You should not shave your underarms or pluck your eyebrows in excess. You may clip your hairs with a pair of scissors. You may clip your hairs to cut down on extreme perspiration. You should never cut your head hairs. You may, however clip your uneven ends.
13. Use only Moorish Bath Compound to douche, if necessary. Do not use chemical feminine sprays, douches or deodorized sanitary napkins or tampons.
14. Chewing gum looks bad and teases the digestive system. If you have to chew gum, you should not do so on the streets.
15. You are not to be outside on the street at night. You should not hang out on the street corners , at pool halls, bars, liquor stores, discos, etc. No matter whether a family member owns one.
16. Always go clean and neat.
17. You should keep your mind clear of bad thoughts.
18. You should wear cotton under pants. Cotton absorbs your sweat and cuts down on vaginal infections that other materials cause.
19. Practice eating two meals per day. As the Prophet teaches us, this is for our own good.
20. When driving in a car with a brother (that is not your husband, father or blood brother) whether he is married or single, you should always be seated in the back.
21. Sleep in appropriate night clothes and teach your children to do likewise.
22. Strive to dress and act feminine. Avoid the appearance of masculinity.
23. We submit to right and righteousness.
24. We ask questions when we don't understand.
25. We are punctual.
26. Brush teeth and comb hair daily.
27. Practice to improve handwriting, cooking, sewing, speaking ability, and computer skills.
28. We talk in soft moderate tones.

29. Wear stockings that are smooth textured and near our skin shade.
30. We have short engagements to avoid falling victim to restrictive law.
31. We wear clothing suitable for weather and season of the year.
32. Salute national on M.G.T. Class day only.
33. Carry complaints and suggestions through the proper channels.
34. Strive to cultivate love and respect for self and others.
35. Visit the sick and shut-ins.
36. We pay charity.
37. We strive to attend Convention.
38. It is not necessary to pray during menstruation.
39. We do not give Believer's phone numbers or addresses to strangers, especially over the phone. Tell them to see the Secretary.
40. We do not permit our children to take liberties in other people's homes.
41. Wearing lace or thin scarves is inappropriate for the Temple.
42. We do not go to any of the devil's amusements, such as movies.
43. We do not wear pointed toe shoes.
44. DO NOT EAT HOG (pig, pork, swine, lard). We do not touch this divinely prohibited flesh.
45. Don't wear sheer or see-though clothes in public.
46. Don't smoke.
47. Don't steal from or fight each other.
48. Don't be quick to jump to conclusions about a person of what he or she says.
49. Don't criticize unjustly without cause.
50. Don't be rude or disrespectful.
51. Don't be careless and neglectful of duties to home or Temple.
52. Don't be quick tempered.
53. Don't be withdrawn and distrustful.
54. Don't be easily persuaded to do wrong by unbelievers, be they relatives or friends.

55. Don't be selfish or evil thinking.
56. Do not bring up problems to the Chairman or Grand Sheik if you can solve them first.
57. Don't give your word unless you are sure you can fulfill it.
58. Don't break the confidence of a sister.
59. Do not stay away from class just because they are not run the way you think they should be.
60. We submit to our husband as long as he is right.
61. We observe ablution before prayer.
62. We practice proper conduct and teach our children the same.
63. We take an interest in anything that may affect our children.
64. We practice the highest forms of health hygiene and sanitation.
65. We save money for future use and unforeseen misfortunes. Strive to avoid credit.
66. Strive to wear white as soon as possible.
67. Pray five times per day, making sure you say the Morning Prayer.
68. Whenever a new sister comes into the Temple, we do our best to make her feel at home.
69. Be gentle, kind, and firm when dealing with sisters.
70. Be clean, neat, and well-groomed at all times, EVEN AROUND THE HOUSE.
71. Think before speaking.
72. Train children to be respectful to all adults, Temple officials, and teachers.
73. Keep an interest in current events/ news.
74. Be careful of leaving doors unlocked when in and out of the house. Also be careful of who you let into the house.
75. A sister looks for the good in a sister instead of harping on the worst.
76. A sister discovers what can be done instead of grumbling about what cannot.
77. A sister draws her strength from a deep belief in Allah and trusts in the Prophet Drew Ali's Teachings.

78. We regard problems, small or large, as opportunities.
79. We push ahead when it would be easy to quit.
80. We accept small gains realizing that the longest journey begins with one step.
81. We accept misunderstandings as the price of sowing the greater good of others.
82. We try to make suggestions for improvements in a constructive manner.
83. We make it a matter of principle to attend all Temple meetings and activities.
84. We fight those who fight with us. But we are never the aggressor.
85. We do not attempt to teach to Asiatics. We ask them to the Temple for official teaching.
86. We do not use aluminum cookware. We use glass, stainless steel, and Corning ware.
87. We do not eat nuts (peanuts, walnuts, etc.)
88. We do not give X-Mas cards or gifts. We give Prophet's Day gifts and cards.
89. We do not use tampons. We use sanitary napkins.
90. We do not go barelegged.
91. We don't date or have boyfriends.
92. We don't flirt with or pursue brothers. We let them pursue us.
93. We don't gossip or spread rumors.
94. We use Clorox for dish washing.
95. Don't wash kitchen line with other clothing. Wash separately.
96. Don't wear slits in skirts. We wear pleats.
97. Don't wear hair curlers in the street.
98. Don't eat tuna or any other fish that weighs over 50lbs.
99. Don't eat fresh baked bread. Wait at least 24hrs before eating it.
100. We don't practice any vices, gambling, swearing, drinking intoxicants, using dope, perverted sex acts, adultery fornication, etc.

Circle 7 Holy Koran – Ch. 30: Charity

How to Keep House

A Thirty Day Program That Will Turn Your House Into a Moslem Home

Islam!

Welcome to the "How To Keep House" area of our Moorish Girls Training and General Civilization Class. How should a Moorish home be kept? Clean, peaceful, and well-repaired. We have learned from the Program designed by our Leader and Prophet, Noble Drew Ali, How to Keep House in this manner. The Moorish home is an example to all, of the highest form of cleanliness. Thirty days after your receive the following instructions on how to achieve your goal (a clean, peaceful, well-repaired home), as a Moorish Sister in the M.S.T. Of A., expect to have your home inspected by designated Sisters within your S.A. These Sisters will come unannounced with checklists in hand to note how you have applied what you have been taught in this class.

Get Rid of Clutter

1. A good housekeeper knows when it is time to throw a thing out.
2. Keeping unnecessary items (old papers and magazines, clothes no one wears, old letters, cards, bottles, bills, toys, dishes, shoes, etc.)
3. If items must be kept, they should be kept neatly in a clearly labeled box.
4. Each thing should have a specific, practical place. For example: Toys can be kept in a toy box in the play area.
5. Some things may need several homes: pencil holders should be placed in the kitchen, at the main telephones and throughout the house where needed.
6. Wicker baskets are great and neat "homes" for things. They can hold pencils in a reception room or study, hair accessories in the bedroom, or combs and brushes in the bathroom. They

are also decorative, look good in almost any home décor, and keep things close to where they will be used.

7. The more convenient it is to put something away, the less likely it is to end up as clutter.

8. Teaching children (or other family members) to put things away can be accomplished by consistent modeling and insistence. Often organizational skills can also be taught in phases.

9. Getting rid of clutter and learning new habits doesn't occur overnight. Start now by not allowing new clutter items to come into your home. Fliers, newspapers, bulletins, school newsletters, letters and bills are examples. Though not all incoming clutter is paper-based, probably over half of it is. Once read or dealt with, anything of simple paper origin can go in the garbage can.

10. A lot of incoming clutter hangs around the house simply because it was not dealt with when it came it arrived.

11. One piece of invaluable advice is to make it a rule to never pick up a piece of paper twice. As much as possible, paper should only end up in your hands once.

12. One piece of invaluable advice is to make it a rule to never pick up a piece of paper twice. As much as possible, paper should only end up in your hands once.

13. Often we read things and then put them away to do later. Later, of course, the entire thing must be sorted out of a pile of other junk and re-read. If things are dealt with immediately (or in the case of bills, put away immediately), then they don't become clutter. Another thing that adds to disorganization and clutter in the home is that many people hang onto paper clutter (and other kinds of clutter as well) because they think they may need it down the road. Most clutter, as long as it has been dealt with, or has served its purpose, can be thrown out.

Day 1

Arm yourself with garbage bags and take a deep breath. Then throw out all unnecessary items. ANYTHING that is NOT ABSOLUTELY NECESSARY for your family's well-being should be thrown out. This is an all day task. The larger the home or family, the more time it will take you to complete this task. You are well on your way to having a clutter-free home.

The Moslem's Courtship

According to the Webster's Dictionary, the word Courtship means: (noun) 1. The act of soliciting favor. 2a. The act of wooing in love; 2b. Solicitation of a woman to marriage.

The definition that relates to this subject is definition 2b. (Solicitation of a woman to marriage.) Solicitation is the act of soliciting. To solicit means to make a request for solicitation.

When a brother see a sister that he thinks will make him a good wife, he should mention this to the Grand Sheik, Sheik, or the Adept. He should first find out if she is available for marriage, then he should be asked to be introduced to this sister in order that they may get better acquainted. If she is available for marriage and desires to get better acquainted with him, it is proper that they correspond with each other by mail or by phone, but they must keep the conversation clean. The sister must never invite the brother to her home unless there will be other (Moslem) adults present. They shouldn't sit together, and must never stare at each other nor touch one another.

Holy Qur'an 24:31

"Say to the Believing women that they lower their gaze....and do not display their adornment except to their husbands, or their fathers, or the fathers of their husbands..."

They should never be alone in a room by themselves. After the brother and sister have gotten better acquainted over a period of time and still decide to marry, the only thing to do then is to set up plans for marriage.

However, Noble Drew Ali instructs the sister to check her prospective husband, not to just take him on the surface level. Check his character, take note of the type of friends he keeps. If possible, find out his family background. Is he an honorable man? Can his word be trusted? Is he able to support a wife? Will he be able to support a family? What is his attitude toward children? There are many important points which a sister must consider in selecting a husband.

Noble Drew Ali also instructs the brother to look for a clean and respectable woman for a good wife; a good homemaker. He should check into the background of the woman he wishes to marry. He may also learn of her character by the people she takes as friends. He must also know if she adheres to the laws of Islam.

Prophet Drew Ali instructs the sister in Islam: *"When a person gets in a hurry, in a just a few days after the hasty marriage they wish that they had never bothered with the person they married. Coldness comes between the two people. Wait for the warm love which Allah (God) brings to true mates."*

HKMSTA Chapter 21, verse 3

Sisters' Auxiliary
Student Class Creed

1. I will strive to control our attentions in order to do a careful and accurate job on our requirements.
2. I will strive to improve my listening skills, take notes, read and think of what is being said and fit it into what I already know.
3. I will strive to review what is taught and keep and overall pattern in mind.
4. I will strive to improve my handwriting through practice because I need ease in handwriting to transfer my thoughts to paper.
5. I will strive to keep a record of assignments and keep homework up to date.
6. I will strive to give a new sister a good impression of Islamism as I realize this is important to help her revive her hidden qualities.
7. I will strive to have a complete notebook and keep it up to date.
8. I will strive to dress and act like the kind of Moslem I wish to become.
9. I will strive to follow instructions, asking questions when I don't understand.
10. I will strive each day to do something to help the Program.

The Uplifting of Fallen Humanity

Our Divine Prophet, Noble Drew Ali consistently appraised all members of the Moorish Science Temple of America that the purpose of said organization was to "Uplift fallen Humanity." The reason was that he wanted all members always to be consciously aware of what our objective is.

Consequently, all members must know what uplifting humanity is and what they must do to be directly involved in the purpose of the Moorish Science Temple of America.

What is the uplifting of fallen humanity?

Uplifting fallen humanity is improving the spiritual, social, and intellectual condition of the Moorish People whose will is not consistent with the will of the Father God, Allah; those who have lost their greatness and are in need of earthly and divine salvation.

What is the current general condition of Moorish Americans?

Indeed, some Moorish Americans are not dealing with their spiritual, social, and intellectual deficiencies effectively and are not classified and treated as undesirable by True American Citizens.

The lives of the Unconscious Moors and unfaithful members of the Moorish Science Temple of America are not based upon the religion and Divine Creed of their forefathers and their Father God-Allah is not pleased with the works that are being performed in North America by unconscious Moors and unfaithful members.

Furthermore, these individuals are not engaged in those actions which will assure them their earthly and divine salvation and enable them to be involved in the uplifting of fallen humanity.

How do we uplift fallen humanity?

It's very simple. We must:

1. Become a member of the Moorish Science Temple of America;
2. Proclaim and practice Love, Truth, Peace, Freedom, and Justice;
3. Send our children to Sunday School and or play an active role in our Moorish Sunday School;
4. Attend our meetings promptly;
5. Pay our obligations and contribute to the Moorish Uplifting fund;

6. Keep in line with the necessities of the Temple;
7. Become a part and parcel of all uplifting Acts of the Moorish Science Temple of America.

How to Take Care of Your Husband

"A wife's mind should be to console her husband's mind."

"She is to do something in the way of making him feel good to go out tomorrow to work. Otherwise, the man is outside looking for peace of mind."

"No man wants a woman home arguing with him."

"Be civilized in asking and telling."

"Woman must always submit and recognize man as the head."

"The worst hell is an icy spirit between husband and wife a home where there is no peace, no love."

"As long as she followed this Divine Law, everything she laid her hands to, He made it prosper."

Words of Elijah Muhammad

COMFORT HIM

The burdens of life weigh heavily upon the shoulders of men since they are responsible for maintaining and supporting their families. In fulfilling this responsibility, the man of the household must confront many problems and obstacles of the home. Some of these problems may be the pressures of work, the hassles of traffic and commuting to and from work, concerns over the issues of the day, and the pressures of trying to improve the living conditions of his family. The amount of pressure upon a responsible man is enormous. It is no wonder that the average lifespan of a man is less than the woman.

In order for the husband to be able to cope with the burdens of life it is necessary to have someone listen to and sympathize with him. He may feel alone and in need of finding refuge and comfort amidst these pressures. It is natural that the man looks towards his wife and family as a source of comfort and relief. Therefore, anticipate his expectations and needs. Be cordial and warm when he first returns home after working. Have refreshments waiting or let him feel you are at his disposal to care for his needs. Try not to overwhelm him with criticizing him the minute you see him. Let him rest and recover his strength before putting up demands of the family's personal issues.

When your husband comes home, have a smile and a warm greeting for him. Attend to his physical needs of fatigue, hunger, and thirst. Then ask him about his problems. If he is willing to talk, be a good listener and sympathize with him. Try to express your genuine concern and then help him realize that the problems are not as impossible and huge as he might think. Give him encouragements of support and help him cope with the issues. You can say something like this: These problems are being faced by many people. With a strong will-power and patience, it is possible to overcome the difficulties as long as one does not let the problems get the better of you. These problems, as a matter of fact, are tests as well as builders of the true character of a person. Do not despair. You can overcome them through determination and perseverance.

At times of difficulty, your husband is in need of your attention and love. You should come to his aid and nurse him. Do not underestimate your ability to soothe and strengthen him. There is no one more devoted and concerned over your husband's well-being than yourself. He would be able to draw strength from your devotions to him and cope with his problems which will relieve his respect and love would also be greater which can only lead towards strengthening your marital relationship.

APPRECIATE HIM

Your husband, like anyone else, enjoys being appreciated. He is willing to support his family and regards it as a moral and lawful obligation. When he is thanked and appreciated for doing his duty, those duties no longer seem to be a burden.

Whenever he buys home appliances or something like clothes or shoes for you and the children, be happy and thank him. Show your gratitude for the trivial things he does such as buying groceries, taking the family on trips and giving you your allowances. By showing your appreciation, you will make your husband feel good and rewarded for the trouble he has taken. Be careful that you do not take his duties for granted and become indifferent towards his contributions to the family. He may become disheartened about the welfare of the family. He may prefer to spend his money elsewhere or on himself.

If a friend or relative presented you with a pair of stockings or a bunch of flowers, you would thank them repeatedly. So it is only natural and fair to show appreciation to your husband for his consideration and thoughtfulness. Do not think that you would be belittling yourself demonstrating your appreciation. On the contrary, you would be loved and cared for more because you appreciate the efforts of your husband whereas snobbism and selfishness can only lead towards great misfortunes.

FORGIVE HIM

A husband and a wife need to be able to forgive each other. If the members of a family are unforgiving and pursue each others mistakes, then either the family will separate or they will experience and unbearable life.

Your husband probably makes mistakes. He may insult you, abuse you, tell lies, he might even hit you. Such acts might be condemned by any man. If your husband, after making a mistake, regrets it or you feel he is regretful himself for his misconduct, then forgive him and do not pursue the matter. If he is regretful but not prepared to express his apologies, then do not try to prove his mistake. Otherwise, he may feel humiliated and he may retaliate by picking out your mistakes and consequently start an on-going battle of unforgiving. So it is better for you to remain silent until he condemns himself from his conscience and starts to feel remorse about it. He would then regard you as a wise and devoted wife who is interested in her husband and family.

BE CLEAN AND BEAUTIFUL

It is customary with most women that whenever they go to a party or a gathering, they wear their best dresses and adorn themselves with the best. However, upon returning home, they take their dresses off and put on an old, shabby dress. These women are not particular about cleanliness at home ad do not beautify themselves. They walk around the house with disheveled hair, stained clothes, and torn socks. In fact, the situation must almost be reverse, that is, a woman should adorn herself at home and charm her husband in order to conquer his heart and in order not to leave any gap for other women to fill.

Winning the heart of a man, especially for a long time, is not easy. Do not think, "He loves me. I don't need to look beautiful for him or try to win his heart or entice him." You must always maintain his love toward yourself. Be sure that your husband would enjoy having a tidy, beautiful, and clean wife, even though he may not express it. If you do not satisfy his inner desires and do not dress attractively at home, he may see beautiful and attractive women outside the house. He may then become disheartened in you and might deviate from the right path. When he sees attractive women, do you think he will be attracted to you? So try to look attractive

THINK OF NO OTHER MAN

Do not think of any men except your husband and find peace with him. If you do otherwise, you will place yourself in a strained condition. Now that your have agreed to live with your husband, why should you be constantly noticing other men? Why should you compare him with others? What do you achieve by looking at other men except putting yourself in a permanently miserable state and cause mental anguish for yourself. Do not make compliments for other men. Do not think of any man other than your husband. Do not think to yourself, "I wish I had married so and so," "I wish my husband looked like...," " I wish my husband's job was...," "I wish...," "I wish...," "I wish...," Why should you imprison yourself with these thoughts? Why should you upset the foundations of your marriage? If any of those wishes had come true, how would you know that you would have been more satisfied? Are you sure that the wives of those so-called "faultless" men are satisfied with them? If your husband suspects that you show interest in other men, he would be disheartened and would at home and be sure that he will not lose interest in you. You must not cut jokes with other men or keep company with them. Men are so sensitive that they cannot even tolerate their wives to show an interest in a picture of another man.

BE WISE IN DEALING WITH IN-LAWS

One of the problems of family life is the one cause between the wife and her husband's relatives. Some women do not have a good relationship with their husband's mother, sisters, or brothers. On the one hand, the wife may try to dominate her husband so that he would not be able to pay any attention even to his mother, or any of his other relatives, and she may try to sow discord between them. On the other hand, her mother-in-law regards herself as the owner of her son and daughter-in-law. The mother tries hard to hold on to her son and is watchful that the new woman does not try to possess him fully. She may fabricate lies about her daughter-in-law or find fault in her. Such an attitude might be followed by many arguments and even occasional hostilities. The situation becomes even worse if they all live in the same house. Even though a problem may occur between two women, the real anguish and distress remains with the man in the middle.

The husband is trapped in an argument where he cannot take sides. On the one hand is his wife who he would like to have an independent life without any interference from outsiders. He naturally feels that he must support her and make her happy. But on the other hand, he thinks of his parents who have helped him with his life, education, and have spent their own lives in bringing him up. He feels that his parents expect him to help them in their times of need and that it would not be fair to abandon them. Besides, if he himself was in need of something, who else, other than his parents, would help him and his family? As a result, he realizes that his best and most trustworthy friends are his parents and relatives.

So, the dilemma for a sensible man is either to choose the wife and abandon the parents, or vice versa, but neither of these is possible.

Consequently, he has to cope with both sides and keep them satisfied which, itself, is a difficult task. The only possible way to ease the situation is that the wife should be loyal and wise. A man in this situation expects his wife to help solve the problem.

If the wife respects her mother-in-law, seeks advice from her, and becomes obedient and friendly with her, then the mother-in-law will be her greatest supporter.

For the sake of your husband and for the sake of your own comfort as well as to find many good friends and supporters, put up with your husband's relatives. Do not be selfish and ignorant; be wise and do not cause you husband any distress.

DO NOT LOOK FOR SHORTCOMINGS

It is the hope of every man and woman to find a spouse who is perfect, but such hopes are unrealistic. It is unlikely to find a woman who regards her husband as perfect.

Those women who are in search of faults in their husbands will undoubtedly find them. They would find a trivial shortcoming and exaggerate it by harping on the matter to the point that it becomes an unbearable impediment. This defect then replaces all the merits of the husband. They always compare their husbands with other men. They have established a so-called ideal man in their imaginations whose standards do not fit in their husbands. Therefore, they are always complaining about the shortcomings in their marriage. The women regard themselves as unfortunates and failures which gradually turn them into spiteful women.

What does such behavior in a woman do to her husband? He may be a very patient person who can tolerate rudeness, but most likely he will become insulted and develop a grudge against her. This would likely lead to mutual arguments and elaborations of the shortcomings in each other.

They will both become contemptuous of each other and their life will turn into a series of arguments. Thus, they will either live in misery together or go for a divorce. In either case, both will lose, especially when there is no guarantee that another marriage may prove otherwise.

Your husband is a human being like you. He is not perfect, but he may have many merits. If you are interested in your marriage and your family, then do not set out to find his weaknesses. Do not regard his small defects as important. Do not compare him with an ideal man whom you have established in your mind. There may be some faults with your husband which are not present in others. But you should remember that other men may have defects which are non-existent in yours. Be satisfied with his merits. You will consequently see that his merits outweigh his faults. Besides, why should you expect a perfect husband when you are imperfect yourself?

Be wise! Stop being frivolous! Ignore the faults and do not mention them in front of or behind your husband. Try to create a warm atmosphere in your family and enjoy the blessings of Allah. However, there may be flaws in your husband's character which you may be able to correct. If so, then you can succeed only by behaving considerately and with patience. You must not criticize him, but approach him in a friendly manner.

The task of a wife is to maintain and take care of a husband. It is not an easy undertaking. Those women who are unaware of this feature of their role, may find difficulty in fulfilling the task. It is a job for the woman who is aware that the job requires a degree of sagacity, style, and ingenuity. For a woman to be a successful wife, she should also provide adequate measures to maintain his health and well-being. The results of her efforts are directed towards making the man into a kind and respected husband who would be a proper guardian for his family, and a good father from whom the children should seek guidance and respect. Allah, the All Knowing, has endowed woman with extraordinary power. The prosperity and happiness as well as the misery of the family are in her hands.

DON'T BE SUSPICIOUS

It is not wrong if a woman is watchful of her husband, but only if it does not exceed to a state of suspicion and mistrust.

A woman of suspicion imagines that her husband is disloyal to her. She suspects him of having an affair with another woman. She loses trust in him because he comes home late or he was seen talking to a woman. If he helps a widow and her children, the wife may think that he has an interest in her other than a charitable one. If any woman gives her husband a compliment, saying that he is handsome or well-mannered, she concludes that he is interested in that woman. Upon finding a strand of hair in his car, she thinks there is another woman in his life.

Such women with these thoughts and inconclusive proof gradually assume certainty regarding their husbands' unfaithfulness. They think about it every day and night. They also tell others—friends and foes—about it, who, in the name of in the name of sympathy, reinforce the allegations and in turn tell the concerned women about other unfaithful men.

Arguments result. Then the woman begins to ignore the affairs of the house and the children and might even go to her parents. She would monitor him and search his pockets. She would read his letters and would explain any trivial matter as due to his unfaithfulness.

With this attitude, she would make the family's life hard and turn the house into a burning hell in which she would also suffer. If her husband brought proof of his innocence, or swore that he had not been committing anything wrong., she would not be satisfied. The family atmosphere changes into an environment or pessimism, suspicion, and constant arguing. The children would suffer and the mental effects are grave.

HELP HIM AVOID PITFALLS

Wise and experienced men know both their friends and their foes. However, there are men who are simple; they can easily be deceived and would be easily influenced by others.

There are people who are imposters and are lying in wait for simple men. The imposter, though pretending to be a good-doer, traps the man and draws him toward corruption. The simple man may not realize his situation for a while, but one day he wakes up and finds himself deep in a trap from which there is no escape.

If you look around yourself, you see tens of such unfortunate people. Perhaps none of them intended to fall into the trap or become corrupt, but through their own simplicity, ignorance, and thoughtlessness, they are now prey upon by the corrupt in society.

On this account, the simple men need to be taken care of. A wise and watchful wife would monitor her husband's activities and watch his associates indirectly without his knowledge, remembering not to directly interfere with the affairs of her husband, or to tell then the "dos" or "don'ts." The reason for this is because men mostly do not like to be treated as a tool in the hands of others. Otherwise, they may react sharply.

Some men, some times, come back home later than usual. If this is the case and the number of late arrivals to home are within an acceptable limit, then there is no need to worry. Men are sometimes engaged in certain unexpected events which they try to pursue after work. However, if the number of late arrivals exceeds the accepted limit, then his wife should make an effort to investigate. But investigation is not easy; it requires patience and wisdom. One must avoid anger or protest. The wife should first of all talk to him softly and kindly. She would ask him why he came home later than the day before and where he has been. Again, she should pursue the matter wisely and patiently.

If she finds that he comes home late because of his work of attends scientific, religious, and moral meetings, then she should leave him alone. If she feels that he has found a new friend, she should find out who he is. If his new friend is a well-mannered person with a clean record, then she should not worry. It is even recommended that she encourages him in his new friendship because a good friend is a great blessing.

If you feel that your husband is going astray or that he is associated with corrupt and unworthy people, then you should stop him immediately. A woman in this situation has a great responsibility. The slightest mishandling of the situation, through carelessness, may shatter their family life. This is a situation where the wisdom and cleverness of some women can become useful and apparent. One should remember that arguments are not the solution and they may result in the exact opposite. A woman, who experiences this event, has two tasks to achieve:

First, she should assess the situation at home; and should examine herself and her attitude. She must find out the reason for her husband's behavior. She should fairly judge why he has grown cold towards his family and gone astray. She may find that her own attitude has been the cause; or perhaps she had been indifferent to his desires for food, her looks or the affairs of the house. Such matters draw men away from home. They may then pursue outside deviant activities in order to forget their problems.

Secondly, she should show him as much kindness as possible. She should advise him and remind him of the grim consequences of his deeds. She should even cry and beg him to give up his bad companions. She must say to him, "I love you from the bottom of my heart. I am proud of you. I prefer you to all thinks and I am ready to devote myself to you. But I am saddened by one thing: why should a man, like you, have these kinds of friends, or attend that kind of party? Such deeds are not suitable for you. Please give them up." The wife must continue this attitude until she conquers the heart of her husband. It is possible that the husband is used to unworthy habits and that he would not be influenced easily, but the wife should not become disappointed. She should pursue her goal with greater strength and patience.

Women have great power and influence over men. She is able to do whatever she wills if she puts her mind to it. If a woman decides to help save her husband from the filth of corruption, she can do it—provided she acts wisely.

THE DIVIDED HOUSE

Husband remains an unbeliever. What is the root of the Problem?

Remember, there are different degrees of unbeliever. Some bitterly persecute the believer. Some constantly nag the believer, trying to break down integrity. Some subtly discourage the believer. Others show indifference towards true worship. Gradual progress can be made in helping the unbeliever in breaking down opposition or in stirring up interest. If the unbeliever is favorable, the believer, with the aid of the Islamic congregation, should work towards the goal of uniting the family by means of the home or Temple study. If the unbeliever is opposed, the believer needs to remember the above statements, about reading the sky and earth.

Matt. 10:32-41

33: Whosoever therefor shall confess me before men, him I will confess also before my Father which art in heaven. But whosoever shall deny me before men, him I will I also deny before my Father which art in heaven.

34: Think not that I am come to send peace on Earth: I come not to send peace, but a sword.

35: For I am come to set man at variance against his father and the daughter against her mother, and the daughter-in-law against her mother-in-law.

36: And a man's foes shall be they of his own household.

37: He that loveth their son or daughter more than me is not worthy of me.

38: And he that taketh not his cross, and followeth after me, is not worthy of me.

39: He that findeth his life shall lose it, and he that loseth his life for my sake shall find it.

40: He that receiveth you receiveth me, and he that receiveth me receiveth Him that sent me.

41: He that receiveth a prophet in the name of a prophet shall receive a prophet's reward; and he that receiveth a righteous man in the name of righteous man shall receive a righteous man's reward. 42: And whosoever shall give to drink unto one of these little ones a cup of cold water only in the name of a disciple, verily I say unto you, he shall in no wise lose his reward.

On the other hand, if the wife keeps on going to meeting, explaining to her unbelieving husband why they are so important to her, he might in time be impressed. May not the unbeliever eventually accept an invitation to attend one of these meetings and thus see for himself their beneficial nature? So the believing mate must always that keeping integrity works for the benefit of not only the Believer, but also of the unbeliever.

Note: Integrity according to *The American Heritage Dictionary* means steadfast adherence to a strict moral or ethical code.

Moorish Girls' Training

How to Rear Our Children

Notes to Remember

1. The Moorish mother is devoted to her children.
2. The Moorish mother teaches her child obedience.
3. The Moorish mother teaches her child from the cradle.
4. The Moorish mother teaches the child the Islamic way of life.
5. The Moorish mother understands that children are equal to adults in terms of human worth and dignity.
6. The Moorish mother concentrates on striving to be upright so that her children will do the same.
7. The Moorish mother does not criticize her children or others so that her children will not learn to condemn.
8. The Moorish mother avoids hostility in order to tone down aggressiveness in her child.
9. The Moorish mother is tolerant in order that her child may learn patience.
10. The Moorish mother gives encouragement so that her child will learn to have confidence.
11. The Moorish mother gives praise so that the child will learn to appreciate.
12. The Moorish mother deals with her child in fairness to help him learn the meaning of justice.
13. The Moorish mother shows her child approval so that he will learn to love himself.
14. The Moorish mother lets her child see a good example.
15. The Moorish mother remembers that she is the "Mother of Civilization."
16. The Moorish mother reads to her children every night a chapter from the Holy Koran of the M.S.T. of A. as a bedtime story.

Obedience

"When you find a house of disobedient children, you will find a house that has a sorrowful spirit. When you find a house with a sorrowful spirit – when this spirit should be as high as the Wisdom of that house, yet the spirit is low – then you find a disobedient house."

Obedience is one of the keys to our success as Moslems. If we were to study the patterns and habits we have formed since being in the Temple, it would be easy to recognize the need for us to study obedience.

Obedience means submission, and Islam means peace and submission, and a Moslem is one who submits entirely to the Will of Allah (God); therefore, to write on obedience is really to write on Islam.

This aspect does of course play an important part, yet it is not the only meaning of obey. To obey also means that there is something planned, written or spoken for us to be guided by – and that something to be guided by is Islam.

To be able to submit to authority, submit to orders, submit to instructions, submit to guidance, submit to jurisdiction of Islam, takes a very good man – especially when it calls for submitting to Asiatic authority. We cannot become good Moslems unless we learn to submit. We will not learn to submit until we learn to obey.

When you find a house of disobedient children, you will find a house that has a sorrowful spirit. When you find a house with a sorrowful spirit – when this spirit should be as high as the Wisdom of that house, yet the spirit is low – then you find a disobedient house. You will find a house that needs to learn the lesson of obedience.

The scripture says, "But if ye will obey the voice of the Lord, bur rebel against the commandments of the Lord, then shall the had of the Lord be against you, as it was against your fathers."

Now who is this 'voice of the Lord' that we will not obey? Who gives us the commandments of the Lord which we rebel against? If we believer that the Prophet Noble Drew Ali is the Prophet of Allah, then he is the 'voice of the Lord' who gives us the commandments from Him. So in our disobedience, we disobey God by disobeying His Prophet, and this puts God against us.

When we are disobedient to Allah's Prophet, Allah will turn us aside, turn us away from Islam, and then we go after vain things which the Book says, "...cannot profit (benefit) us nor deliver what we seek..." for they are the vain things we seek if we seek not to obey Allah's Prophet.

When we accept Islam as our way of life, then we become precious in the eyes of Allah and His Prophet. When we disobey, the scripture says, "We have played the fool, and have erred exceedingly." When we do not obey Allah and his Prophet, they take away from us the things we desire.

When we have not been blessed for long periods of time, there is no one to blame but ourselves. If we were to examine self, we would find that somewhere along the line, we have been disobedient to that which we know is the right way.

The Holy Qur'an so beautifully teaches us: "And we sent to no Messenger but that he should be obeyed by Allah's Command." This tells us that Allah, God Himself, commands us to obey His Prophet. Our obedience is not without reward. The Holy Qur'an further says, "And whoever obeys Allah and The Messenger, they are those upon whom Allah has bestowed favors from among the prophets and the truthful and the faithful and the righteous, and a goodly company are they."

This teaches us that our obedience makes us to become companions of the Prophet and teaches us that in our obedience, we learn to understand the truth. Our faith becomes true, and we become righteous men and good Moslems and men whose company we should keep.

Surely, Prophet Noble Drew Ali has revealed to us a great truth which is good for us all when we obey it. Whoever follows this truth does it for his own good, and whoever makes an error and refuses to obey this truth and goes against it, he makes an error which is only to his detriment.

The Holy Qur'an says, "O would that we had obeyed Allah and His Messenger." This is because Allah gives them a double chastisement and curses them with a great curse for their disobedience; and because they seek to follow this world's life instead of that which leads them to the Hereafter.

Of course there have always been those who are obedient and those who are not. Usually those who refuse to be obedient become fascinated with this life instead of looking forward to the Hereafter. Because of this, Allah leaves them remaining in error and the Holy Qur'an says that this is their just due.

The Holy Qur'an says, "And certainly we raised in every Nation a Messenger saying: Serve Allah and shun the devil. Then of them was he whom Allah guided, and one of them was he whose remaining in error was justly due."

We are blessed to have a Messenger, The Prophet Drew Ali, raised in our Nation and teaching us to serve Allah and shun the devil and his world and his life. Some of us obey these Teachings and Allah guides us on the right path, while others will not heed the Teachings and they remain in error.

These are the ones who seek everything for themselves and nothing for their brother. They are prone to jealousy and they are greedy. They are not following the right path though they look good to the naked and non-understanding eye.

The Holy Qur'an teaches on the one called Korah. It says Korah's wealth and his desires of personal importance led him to ruin. Korah was given great wealth and treasures. He had so much wealth hoarded until the weight if it all would weigh down a strong man, according to the scripture.

The Holy Qur'an says, "The keys of his treasures (not just his money, but his greed and his desires for importance and his refusal to accept and give Praise to Allah) formed a load for 300 mules.

This is exactly how some of us desire to form a load or burden to put upon the shoulders of our Prophet in hopes that the burden will be too great and we in turn can tear down the strength of the Prophet of Allah.

We take our wealth and refuse to give to the cause. We take our time and refuse to give it to the cause. We take the law and break it as often as possible. We take the Teachings and we add to its meanings to satisfy our own desires. We take instead of obeying and giving of ourselves.

The Holy Qur'an says that Korah referred to his wealth and the seemingly exalting position he had, and said that he had been given theses things only on account of the knowledge he had, not realizing Allah is All-Wise and All-Knowing.

So his wealth and attitude about himself was so great (he thought) until he began to exalt himself and not Allah. He forgot Allah and the Will of God, just as we often seek this world's life and forget Allah and the doing of His will as taught by Noble Drew Ali.

This picture of Korah makes reference to our desires in the accumulation of wealth and our desire to build our personal selves as the great object of our life, while we neglect our duty to the truth and refuse to build up with the Prophet of Allah a Nation of people and individuals.

So Korah went forth among the people with great finery, looking for the people to pay homage to him instead of encouraging them to Praise Allah and thank Him for guidance through His Prophet.

Korah was disobedient. He refused to obey that which he had been taught. He forgot where all gifts come from, and he forgot the Giver of Gifts and the reasons we receive these gifts.

But those who had knowledge, those who were wise, those whose understanding lead them to obey Allah's commandments, knew that Allah's reward is better for him who believes and does good than all the money, power, and position we can muster in a decaying world. And they knew that none is made to receive this reward except the patient and the obedient.

Therefore, Korah died and he had no help against Allah's Wrath. His wealth could not defend him He could not plea saying, "I have been your obedient servant." He could not say to Allah, "Show me your mercy," for he had exalted himself. Korah was not obedient, therefore he had understanding.

The Holy Qur'an asks this question: "Do men think they will be left alone on the saying "We believe, and will not be tried?" Just to say we believe and then we will not obey the belief, but yet we get away with this false display of belief. This will give you a false sense of security which leads to temptation, which causes us to disobey and break the law.

But let us remember, the Holy Qur'an says, "Woe to the cheaters! Who when they take the measure (of their dues) from men, take it fully. And when they measure out to others or weigh out for them, they give less than is due.

Obey Allah and obey His Servant (Holy Qur'an). As it is written: "Those who say that they believe and go out saying they disbelieve."

Disobedience comes from the hypocrites and they learn from chastisements. To disobey Allah and His Prophets is actually an act of rebellion against them. And who can rebel against Allah and His Prophet and be successful?

Therefore, only one who does not understand would be foolish enough to believe that he can be disobedient and his actions and deeds will go undetected and not be answered by Allah and His Prophet.

We may feel that because we are not confronted with every act of disobedience at the very time we disobey, that we are getting away with something, but if we recall our Teachings (that every man's deeds cling to his neck – becoming part of his book that weights his life on the scale of the righteous and obedient), we would know how wise it is to obey Allah and His Prophet.

Many wish for us to believe that they will obey Allah, but they will not obey His Prophet. This is because they do not believe in Allah as they say, because they do not see Him, nor do they know Him.

This is because they have no understanding and they have no fear of Allah.

How foolish can we be to say that there is a difference in obeying Allah and in obeying His Prophet?

Remember Lot's Wife

We are living in a glorious time in the history of the Moorish Science Temple of America. Still, there are those who close their eyes to the magnificent work of Prophet Noble Drew Ali. They close their eyes to the time in which we live, for if they could really see, they would not continue on their downward road. The so-called non-believers would forget their excuses and accept Islam, and the professed believer would put forth a greater effort to be upright. Our people are much like Lot's wife (Genesis, Ch. 19). Lot's wife was in the presence of God's angels (messengers); the presence of

God's angels (messengers); she heard their warning and was given an opportunity to escape the destruction of Sodom.

When she looked back upon the burning city, she committed two grave sins: she disobeyed Allah's command, and she showed that she was attracted to that which opposed Allah.

No one has sympathy for Lot's wife. No one identifies with Lot's wife. But upon closer examination, you will see yourself in Lot's wife!

'See yourself,' Asiatic brother and sister, allowing the dead world to supply excuses for your to reject your salvation. 'See yourself,' processing believer, returning to "do your thing" a few more times. 'See yourself,' professed believer, engaging in acts of disregard for the Laws of Allah as taught by the Prophet Noble Drew Ali.

Because Allah did not turn you into a pillar of salt when you first looked back to the dead world, you think you are getting by? You are turning yourself into something of no value to anyone. You are fuel for hell fire.

Certainly, Allah knows if you sincerely try to resist temptation and live an upright life. On the other hand, He knows if you are taking part of the Prophet's teaching as play, and if you foolishly find glamor in the world.

Islam is that which is one the rise, founded on self-evident truths, leading us to everlasting. The one you cling to is being consumed in the fire of Allah's chastisements. The Moorish Science Temple of America will continue to move forward as Lot did, and Mohammad will triumph!

Remember Lot's wife.
Remember the consequences of her actions.

Temple Manners

1. The first point is that the Temple is not a social meeting place. Heads turned to look for friends in the congregation, sleeping, moaning, nods and smiles, gay greetings and distracted restlessness are all out of place in the Temple.
2. If one happens to catch a friend's eye, certainly there is no reason to withhold a glance of recognition and a short smile, but respect for the Temple and concentration on the Sheik should be the basis of all one's behavior.
3. A Moslem sister should never enter the Temple unless she is sure she is properly dressed in the way she has been taught in this booklet.
4. Never hold unnecessary conversations in the check room (voices carry).
5. Relieve self and children before entering the congregation so as not to distract the Sheik who is speaking with entering and leaving. If one must leave their seat, they should place their hand over their heart while getting up and exit that way with a modest bow until out of sight.
6. Teach children to be on best behavior while at the Temple. Quietness in voice and walking should be taught first, with proper guidance. Attentiveness should be taught later.
7. Mother should never leave child unattended if not properly trained. Start training at a very early age.

Mother Love

By Divine Providence, nature has implemented an enduring mother love and affection for her offspring, and causes her to give part of her life to nourish and sustain it until it has arrived at a stage of self-support. Day and night, with unbounded patience and tender, unceasing care and affection she supports and protects the feeble infant during its helpless condition. By her example and teaching, the character of the child has stamped upon it the characteristics of the mother.

It is the mother who gives life to all the people of the world and molds the character of the men who from and rule the communities in which we live. As men, they are largely what their mothers have made them. A child that is born of a good mother and trained up in the way it should go, up to the age of 12 years, in all probability will not depart from it when he is old. Whenever we hear or read of a real man who has accomplished something of real worth, we can be sure he had an exceptional mother And thus the world is indebted for most of its goodness to the mother love implanted by nature to improve the world through her example and teachings of her offspring.

In the lower order of living creatures, the mother love and affection for her offspring is the same, to a degree. The offspring are impelled by nature to follow without reason the example of the mother life. This is called instinct. They do as the mother did. In catching mice, the kitten does not have to be taught. In building a nest, the young build as the mother did in the species to which she belongs.

The Law of Islamism in America

H.K.C.7. Chapter XXVIII

1. "Repine not, O man at the state of servitude: it is the appointment of Allah, and hath many advantages; it removeth thee from cares and solicitudes in life."

2. "The honor of a servant is his fidelity; his highest virtues are submission and obedience."

3. "Be patient, therefore, under the reproofs of thy master, and when he rebuketh thee, answer not again. The silence of thy resignation shall not be forgotten."

H.K.C.7. Chapter XXXVII

1. "Vaunt not thy body because it was first formed; nor of thy brain, because therein thy soul resideth. Is not the master of the house more honorable than its walls?"

2. "The ground must be prepared before corn is planted; the potter must build his furnace before he can make his porcelain."

H.K.C.7. Chapter XXXVIII

1. "The blessing, O man of thy external part, are health, vigor and proportion. The greatest of these is health. What health is to thy body, even that is honesty to the soul."

2. "That thou hast a soul is of all knowledge the most certain, of all truths the most plain unto thee. Be meek, be grateful for it. Seek not to know it perfectly. It is inscrutable."

3. "Thinking, understanding, reasoning, willing, call not these the soul. They are its actions, but they are not its essence."

H.K.C.7. Chapter XXXIX

3. "Learn to esteem as thou ought; then art thou near the pinnacle of wisdom."

4. "Think not with the fool, that nothing is more valuable; nor believe with the pretended wise, that thou oughtest to condemn it. Love it not for thyself, but for the good of others."

5. "Gold cannot buy it for thee, neither mines of diamonds purchase back the moment thou hast now lost it. Employ the succeeding ones in virtue."

H.K.C.7. Chapter XLII

1. "Vain and inconsistent as thou art, O child of imperfection, hoe canst thou be weak? Is not inconsistency connected with frailty? Can there be vanity without infirmity? Avoid the danger of the one, and thou shalt escape the mischiefs of the others."

Sister Pearl Drew Ali, First Consort/Wife of the Prophet Noble Drew Ali circa 1928

Sister Pearl Drew Ali, First Consort/ Wife of the Noble Prophet Drew Ali and Sis. Juanita Richardson Bey. Circa 1928

Women of the Nation of Islam in assembly, July 26, 1963
Source http://fineartamerica.com/featured/african-american-women-dressed-in-white-everett.html

Muslim Girls' Training of the Nation of Islam.
Pictured foreground, Sis. Ethel Sharrief, Chicago, IL
Photo by Gordon Parks 1963

Moorish Sisters at Conference in Chicago, 2006.
Source http://www.ruthsadiel.com/truthinrhyme/id8.html

Sisters' Auxiliary of M.S.T. of A. Temple # 11, Philadelphia 2013

Other Titles Available from Califa Media Publishing

77 Amazing Facts About the Moors with Complete Proof

Applied Solutions for Moorish Nationals: Securing National Interests Through Home Schooling

Isonomi: The Great Masonic Secret: Master Keys

Holistic Philosophy 101

Moorish Children's Guide to History and Culture

Moorish Jewels: Emerald Ed

Moors in America

Mysteries of the Silent Brotherhood of the East, aka The Red Book/ Sincerity

Nationality, the Order of the Day

Noble Drew Ali Plenipotentiaries

Official Proclamation of Real Moorish American Nationality

Well, Come to Klanada

Califa Uhuru Series

Vol. 1: Holy Koran of the Moorish Holy Temple of Science, Circle 7

Vol. 2: "I'm Going to Repeat Myself.": A Collection of Artifacts Authored by Noble Prophet Drew Ali and the M.S.T. of A.

Vol. 3: Mysteries of the Silent Brotherhood of the East a.ka. The Red Book, a.k.a. Sincerity

Vol. 4: Califa Uhuru; A Collection of Literature from the Moorish Science Temple of America

www.ingramcontent.com/pod-product-compliance
Lightning Source LLC
Chambersburg PA
CBHW060342080526
44584CB00013B/880